Greater Than a Tourist Bers

I think the series is wonderful and   ~urists to get
information before visiting the city.

-Seckin Zumbul, Izmir Turkey

I am a world traveler who has read many trip guides but this one really
made a difference for me. I would call it a heartfelt creation of a local
guide expert instead of just a guide.

-Susy, Isla Holbox, Mexico

New to the area like me, this is a must have!

-Joe, Bloomington, USA

This is a good series that gets down to it when looking for things to do
at your destination without having to read a novel for just a few ideas.

-Rachel, Monterey, USA

Good information to have to plan my trip to this destination.

-Pennie Farrell, Mexico

Aptly titled, you won't just be a tourist after reading this book. You'll
be greater than a tourist!

-Alan Warner, Grand Rapids, USA

Thank you for a fantastic book.

-Don, Philadelphia, USA

Helena Cochran

Great ideas for a port day.
-Mary Martin USA

Even though I only have three days to spend in San Miguel in an upcoming visit, I will use the author's suggestions to guide some of my time there. An easy read - with chapters named to guide me in directions I want to go.
-Robert Catapano, USA

Great insights from a local perspective! Useful information and a very good value!
-Sarah, USA

This series provides an in-depth experience through the eyes of a local. Reading these series will help you to travel the city in with confidence and it'll make your journey a unique one.
-Andrew Teoh, Ipoh, Malaysia

Tourists can get an amazing "insider scoop" about a lot of places from all over the world. While reading, you can feel how much love the writer put in it.
-Vanja Živković, Sremski Karlovci, Serbia

GREATER THAN A TOURIST – PORTSMOUTH HAMPSHIRE ENGLAND

50 Travel Tips from a Local

Helena Cochran

Helena Cochran

Cover Image: https://pixabay.com/en/spinnaker-tower-portsmouth-england-713792/

Greater Than a Tourist
Visit our website at www.GreaterThanaTourist.com

Lock Haven, PA
All rights reserved.
ISBN: 9781976946257

>TOURIST

50 TRAVEL TIPS FROM A LOCAL

Helena Cochran

BOOK DESCRIPTION

Are you excited about planning your next trip?

Do you want to try something new?

Would you like some guidance from a local?

If you answered yes to any of these questions, then this Greater Than a Tourist book is for you. Greater Than a Tourist- Portsmouth, Hampshire, England, by Helena Cochran offers the inside scoop on Portsmouth, England. Most travel books tell you how to travel like a tourist. Although there is nothing wrong with that, as part of the Greater Than a Tourist series, this book will give you travel tips from someone who has lived at your next travel destination.

In these pages you'll discover advice that will help you throughout your stay. This book will not tell you exact addresses or store hours but instead will give you excitement and knowledge from a local that you may not find in other smaller print travel books.

Travel like a local. Slow down, stay in one place, and get to know the people and the culture. By the time you finish this book, you will be eager and prepared to travel to your next destination.

Helena Cochran

TABLE OF CONTENTS

10. CATCH THE WATERBUS TO AN AWARD WINNING NAVAL MUSEUM

11. TOUR THE HARBOUR

12. GET YOUR ADRENALINE FIX ON THE WATER

13. ENJOY A DELICIOUS SUNDAY CLASSIC - ROAST DINNER

14. HOP ON BOARD THE LITTLE GREEN FERRY

15. EXPLORE SOME UNDERWATER HISTORY

16. ENJOY PRIME SUNSET VIEWS FROM THE COMFORT OF A PUB

17. TAKE A DAY TRIP TO THE ISLE OF WIGHT

18. TAKE A GUIDED WALK AROUND THE AREA

19. CATCH A GAME OF FOOTBALL AT FRATTON PARK

20. WHERE TO GO SHOPPING IF YOU AREN'T SO INTERESTED IN DESIGNER LABELS

21. HAVE A BEACH DAY

22. GO FOR A RUN

23. GET YOUR SKATES ON

24. LET OUT YOUR INNER CHILD ON THE AMUSEMENT PIERS

25. SEE SOUTHSEA'S VERY OWN BEACH

26. GO BRUNCHING AT SOUTHSEA BEACH CAFÉ

27. BECOME KING OF THE (SOUTHSEA) CASTLE

28. PAY A VISIT TO THE TRANSFORMED HOTWALLS STUDIOS

49. SEE THE LOCAL CATHEDRALS - THE HIGHEST FORM OF CHRISTIAN CHURCHES

50. ENJOY SOME COUNTRY AIR

TOP REASONS TO BOOK THIS TRIP

> TOURIST

GREATER THAN A TOURIST

> TOURIST

GREATER THAN A TOURIST

DEDICATION

This book is dedicated to my parents, for bringing me up in such a great place, and to my travel buddy Molly, who has definitely read this book more than she would have chosen to…

Helena Cochran

ABOUT THE AUTHOR

Helena Cochran is a traveler who has lived around the world (currently in a car in New Zealand), but hails from Gosport, England. Helena loves to surf, create, and explore new places, particularly when the sea is involved. Travel is one of her main passions and she has been to five continents so far, but has plenty more of the world still left to discover.

Helena grew up in Gosport, the town on the peninsular across the harbour from Portsmouth. Whilst that isn't technically Portsmouth, Portsmouth is the city that she uses as reference when asked where she comes from. Growing up, the little green Gosport Ferry that shuttled people and their bicycles to and from Portsmouth, was viewed as her main link to civilisation and entertainment, and she is therefore very familiar with the many attractions of this seaside city.

Helena Cochran

HOW TO USE THIS BOOK

The Greater Than a Tourist book series was written by someone who has lived in an area for over three months. The goal of this book is to help travelers either dream or experience different locations by providing opinions from a local. The author has made suggestions based on their own experiences. Please do your own research before traveling to the area in case the suggested places are unavailable.

Helena Cochran

FROM THE PUBLISHER

Traveling can be one of the most important parts of a person's life. The anticipation and memories that you have are some of the best. As a publisher of the Greater Than a Tourist book series, as well as the popular 50 Things to Know book series, we strive to help you learn about new places, spark your imagination, and inspire you. Wherever you are and whatever you do I wish you safe, fun, and inspiring travel.

Lisa Rusczyk Ed. D.
CZYK Publishing

Helena Cochran

OUR STORY

Traveling is a passion of the "Greater than a Tourist" series creator. Lisa studied abroad in college, and for their honeymoon Lisa and her husband toured Europe. During her travels to Malta, an older man tried to give her some advice based on his own experience living on the island since he was a young boy. She was not sure if she should talk to the stranger but was interested in his advice. When traveling to some places she was wary to talk to locals because she was afraid that they weren't being genuine. Through her travels, Lisa learned how much locals had to share with tourists. Lisa created the "Greater Than a Tourist" book series to help connect people with locals. A topic that locals are very passionate about sharing.

Helena Cochran

WELCOME TO

> TOURIST

Helena Cochran

INTRODUCTION

"The world is a book and those who do not travel read only one page." - Augustine of Hippo

Portsmouth is one of the world's best-known ports and has grown, since Roman times, to become a city providing culture, entertainment, and miles of coastline. As the UK's only island city, it's ideal waterfront location on the south coast of England helps it to deliver a true British seaside experience.

Alongside beach related activities, Portsmouth has on offer an abundance of Naval history that comes from its long and proud maritime heritage. The city has had strong literary connections for centuries, and to this day it continues to nurture creativity and the arts. In addition, the city is known for the cosmopolitan hub of Gunwharf Quays, where you can shop, eat, and drink to your hearts content.

For a small island, Portsmouth really packs in the attractions! My top 50 suggestions are laid out below, ranging from eating pies in a record store, to a water-based treasure hunt - you are sure to find something for every age and budget.

Helena Cochran

1. CHECK OUT PORSMOUTH FROM ABOVE

The Emirates Spinnaker Tower is probably the most recognizable tourist attraction in Portsmouth, visible from water and land. It is so named as it is shaped to resemble a spinnaker sail on a boat, in an ode to Portsmouth's water based history.

At 560 feet high and with three observation decks, the tower offers amazing views across the harbour and the sea. There is a well-designed display that goes around the windows, pointing out landmarks and explaining what you are looking at. The top viewing floor is open to the elements as the roof is made only of a wire mesh, so be warned - you will get wet if it is raining! The lowest viewing deck of the three has a glass floor that you can walk over - if you're brave enough.

There are a few different ways to take in the tower. Either from the ground (free!), with general entry, with a guided tour, or with a drink of prosecco in hand. The guided tours run at 11am and 3pm daily and come with a free guidebook included. The 'Tower and Sparkles' package includes a reserved table in The Clouds and mini bottle of prosecco alongside general entry to the tower.

For the more adventurous amongst you, it is also possible to experience the tower from the outside of it, specifically by abseiling down 100m of it! Packages can include Go Pro footage of the event - certainly a novel way to say that you have visited Portsmouth.

The tower has two cafés; the Waterfront Café is located in the base of the tower, looking out over the harbour, and The Clouds is located 105m up the tower, with an even more extensive view of the harbour. The Clouds just serves drinks and cakes, whereas the Waterfront Café serves cold lunches as well.

2. SATISFY YOUR INNER SHOPAHOLIC IN GUNWHARF QUAYS

The Emirates Spinnaker Tower sits within the Gunwharf Quays Shopping Outlet, which is located on the Portsmouth waterfront. Gunwharf Quays is another big draw for Portsmouth, as people visit from far afield to pick up some bargains at one of the outlet's many designer stores. There are more than 90 stores to choose from, featuring many of Britain's best known brands.

In addition to the shopping possibilities, Gunwharf is also home to over 30 restaurants, bars and cafés. The variety of eateries available is as broad as that of the shops; you can choose from upscale dining at Loch Fyne to popular British café chain Pret a Manger.

Besides shopping and eating, there are also activities on offer as Gunwharf Quays is home to a cinema, bowling alley, art gallery and casino, making Gunwharf perfect for rainy days.

3. LOOK BACK ON PORTSMOUTH FROM ONE OF THE ISLANDS BUILT TO PROTECT IT

From the coastline in Portsmouth, you will be able to see four circular forts out at sea. They were built in the mid 1800's as protection against a seaborne attack. Three of the forts; Spitbank Fort, No Man's Fort, and Horse Sand Fort, are now privately owned and operated as luxury destinations.

Spitbank Fort operates as a 'luxury island retreat' and is the most decadent of the three. An overnight stay there includes a champagne reception, luxury buffet lunch, five course dinner, and a full English breakfast. They also have a bar, pool, sauna and a rooftop perfect for sunbathing - if the English weather permits it. You will also get to have a tour of the historic venue whilst there.

No Man's Fort is a hotel where all of the rooms have sea views (well, you are on a circular fort in the middle of the sea!) and in addition to a tour of the fort you will be provided with drinks, dinner and breakfast. No Man's Fort also has a bunch of bars (including a cabaret bar), a games room, a laZer battle arena (?!), sauna and spa, rooftop hot tubs and a fire pit. Oh, and there's a lighthouse! Pretty cool.

Last up is Horse Sand Fort, which has been preserved as a museum that lets you step back in time. Visitors can explore around 100 restored chambers in the fort, and learn about the naval history surrounding it.

If a nightly package isn't in your travel budget, then another option to consider is the Sunday lunch package, operating at Spitbank and No Man's Fort (Spitbank is the more expensive, more exclusive option - you get champagne). The price includes the boat transfer which will pick you up from Gunwharf Quays, and you will get the whole afternoon on the fort in order to explore the historic site.

4. SEE THE CITY FROM THE WATER

Portsmouth is known for its sailing, and it is surrounded by harbours and marinas. The America's Cup has been hosted in Portsmouth more than once, and Sir Ben Ainslie chose to locate the Landrover BAR (his America's Cup team) headquarters there in a very recognisable development right on the waterfront - it's the big building with a massive union jack on the front of it! So, what better way to explore it that under sail? Gunwharf Quays Marina is situated right at the base of the Spinnaker Tower, with a fantastic location right next to the shops, bars and restaurants of Gunwharf Quays. If you are a sailer yourself then it is possible to moor up here for a few hours, a few days or even a few weeks.

If you aren't lucky enough to have a yacht yourself, but would love to experience the sea air in your hair, then this is still a good place to start a sailing adventure. There are companies offering sailing experiences leaving from Gunwharf that come with professional skippers so you just have to sit back and relax.

You can plan your own itinerary, and a popular option is to explore the naval history around Portsmouth. For example, you can sail to the spot where the Mary Rose sank (which is now in dry dock in the historic dockyard), or you can sail to Buckler's Yard, which is where Nelson's navy warships were built.

.

5. CAST OFF TO CATCH SOME FISH FOR DINNER

There is a vast array of companies offering fishing charters in and around Portsmouth. Whether you are an experienced fisherman, or interested in trying it for the first time, you will be able to find a trip to suit you. Rods and equipment are generally included so don't worry if you're travelling light.

Around Portsmouth, you are able to choose from reef fishing, rough ground fishing, and wreck fishing. Reefs provide excellent deep sea fishing opportunities, and you can generally find pollock, cod and bass. The seabed around Portsmouth varies enormously for rough ground fishing and provides natural food for fish, attracting bream and other varieties of fish. There are also many great wrecks that are accessible with a fishing charter from Portsmouth (or just across the water in Gosport).

If you are feeling more adventurous, then it is also possible to get a two-day fishing trip that takes you over to the French coast, where a wider variety of fish can be found. You can even choose to go for up to five days, on a trip that takes you over to the Channel Islands.

For those of you on more of a tight budget, why not try your hand at crabbing around the seafront in Portsmouth. All you need is a crabbing line, some bait (any kind of meat will work), and a bucket. When you are finished, you can easily release the crabs back into the water where you found them. If you are planning to eat them, then make sure that you check they are of an edible variety, and also that none of them have died before you clean and cook them, as when they die they release a poison through their bodies.

6. INDULGE YOUR ARTISTIC SIDE

Portsmouth is home to a large creative community, so it is definitely worth checking out some art while you are in town. Aspex is a contemporary art gallery, located in Gunwharf Quays, that has multiple exhibition spaces; their focus is on newly emerging artists. Past success stories include Helen Chadwick and Richard Wilson.

Aspex not only run exhibitions but also help to support artists, such as through their Aspex Artists Associates (AAA) scheme. In addition, they have a shop and run talks and seminars throughout the year. Aspex is a cool space to stop by and gain some inspiration to get your creative juices flowing.

Alongside the contemporary gallery, there are many other fine art galleries with a variety of artworks available. If you are looking for a souvenir then there are many local paintings, prints, and graphic prints available to buy.

7. GO FOR DRINKS ON THE WATERFRONT IN GUNWHARF

Gunwharf Quays is known for its reduced price shops, but its waterfront location also provides the perfect location for a few drinks. The bars are popular on a sunny afternoon, and most evenings.

You can find a variety of suitable locations; one option is to go for one of the bars on the first floor of Gunwharf and sit on the balcony. This gives you a great view out over the water where you can watch the little green ferry coming and going from Gosport straight in front of you and you can see the catamaran and car ferries departing for the Isle of Wight to the left. Sometimes you will get to see one of the big

21

Helena Cochran

car ferries coming or going from France - there is always something to see on this section of waterfront.

You can also choose to sit downstairs, either inside or right outside of one of the bars, where you will have the same great views. The bars along the waterfront at Gunwharf mostly look out onto the marina, so you can admire some lovely yachts while watching the world go by.

There are also more drinking options if you follow the waterfront around to the left and walk alongside the canal that cuts through Gunwharf quays. While not right on the seafront, there are some popular bars here and even an old English pub, which is perfect on days when the weather is less favourable.

8. LEARN ABOUT THE NAVAL HISTORY OF PORTSMOUTH

Portsmouth Historic Dockyard is a must visit if you are in the area. You have to pay an entry fee to enter the dockyard, and from there you have access to a multitude of attractions.

One of the most popular attractions is the Mary Rose, who sits in dry dock in a purpose-built museum inside the dockyard. Referred to as 'Britain's version of Pompeii', she was recovered from the seabed in 1982 and has since been painstakingly restored. The Mary Rose is in fact the only 16th Century warship on display anywhere in the world and the museum also showcases an impressive display of artefacts to really bring this period of time to life.

You will probably already have spotted HMS Victory - a very impressive historic warship that sits outside in dry dock by the harbour. She is another dockyard attraction, and it is possible to actually walk on board and explore parts of the ship, alongside an audio guide that explains the remarkable history of the Royal Navy's most famous warship.

The HMS Warrior 1860 also sits in the National Museum of the Royal Navy within the dockyard. Another historic ship, brilliantly restored, that you are allowed to go on board and explore.

An alternative highlight in the dockyard that must be mentioned is Action Stations. Action Stations is an 'interactive indoor attraction', perfect for families to have some fun. There are loads of activities available, including the highest indoor climbing tower in the UK, simulators and even a ninja course (suitable for adults as well as children...). I hope you're feeling energetic!

9. GET LOST IN A TREASURE TROVE OF ANTIQUES

Once inside the Historic Dockyard, you will also find some shops and cafés. The Antiques Storehouse is well worth a visit, and although it is located within the dockyard, it is not necessary to purchase an entry ticket to gain access. The shop is a real old fashioned antiques and collectables shop, crammed full of various treasures. They estimate that they have 10,000 items in the shop so far!

The Antiques Storehouse specialises particularly in marine items, militaria and vintage toys, but has plenty of other stock to keep you busy rummaging through for a couple of hours. The shop is often referred to as a museum in itself, helped by the fact that the building that it is located in was built in 1782. In fact, it is the largest antiques centre on the South Coast of the United Kingdom.

10. CATCH THE WATERBUS TO AN AWARD WINNING NAVAL MUSEUM

Explosion Museum sits across the water from Portsmouth in Priddy's Hard, Gosport. It is accessible by road, but also included in the waterbus from Portsmouth Historic Dockyard if you have purchased an all entry ticket.

The museum is located inside 18th century buildings that were formerly an armaments depot for the Royal Navy. Priddy's Hard was perfectly located on the other side of Portsmouth Harbour to the Dockyard, which made it a safe place to store gunpowder and other ammunition. Nowadays, the museum also has a café, which is a great spot from which to look out on the original 18th century camber dock.

Explosion museum traces the evolution of firepower in the UK, right through until the modern day. There is lots to learn - particularly about big bangs! It covers all kinds of Naval weapons, including mines and torpedoes, and you can take your time to walk around and enjoy the exhibits at your own pace. Even if you are not a big weapons fan, the museum have made the exhibition very creative and enjoyable for all.

11. TOUR THE HARBOUR

Harbour tour boat trips operate from both the dockyard and Gunwharf Quays, and they are a great way to get to know a bit about Portsmouth from the water. They last up to an hour and you will get the opportunity to see whichever navy ships are in port on that day.

In addition, the tours include a full tour of the dockyard, with a live commentary. There is a great view of the Emirates Spinnaker Tower from across the harbour. Portsmouth Harbour really packs in the attractions, and you will also get to see the fortifications that were built to protect Portsmouth over the years; for example the Solent Forts that were described previously, and The Round Tower at the harbour entrance.

Helena Cochran

12. GET YOUR ADRENALINE FIX ON THE WATER

There are a few companies offering RIB trips and experiences departing from Gunwharf Quays, or RIB charters - with or without a skipper - if you are feeling a bit more independent. The experiences range from 20 minute blasts to 60 minute rides.

RIB stands for Rigid Inflatable Boat, basically a powerboat, and a ride on one of these is a fast paced and adrenaline packed way to explore the water around Portsmouth.

A unique experience on offer from Solent Rib Charter is their RIB treasure hunts. They have put together a challenge that sees you racing across the water with your high tech treasure hunting tools, to various destinations on the Isle of Wight, whilst in competition with at least one other team on another RIB. When completed, make sure that you stick around for the Pimms fuelled prize giving ceremony afterward.

13. ENJOY A DELICIOUS SUNDAY CLASSIC - ROAST DINNER

If you are an international visitor to England then a Sunday roast dinner should of course be on your list. The traditional family meal cooked and eaten every Sunday – particularly in the winter - consists of roasted meat (often chicken or beef, but other varieties including veggie options exist), crispy roast potatoes, Yorkshire puddings, stuffing, veggies, and proper gravy.

For those familiar with Sunday roasts, I am sure that you will also agree that it is an excellent activity for a Sunday lunchtime. There are many pubs and restaurants around Portsmouth offering roast dinners on Sunday so have a look around your area. I recommend The Old Customs House in Gunwharf Quays; great food in a cosy, traditional setting.

14. HOP ON BOARD THE LITTLE GREEN FERRY

If you have already arrived in Portsmouth then you will probably have noticed the white and green ferry that shuttles across from the harbour every 15 minutes. This little icon of local history takes foot passengers (and their bicycles) on the short crossing to the town of Gosport across the water. It runs to a very regular schedule, leaving every 15 minutes all day long, and every 7.5 minutes at rush hour, and has a consistently friendly crew who have a tendency to look very alike.

Admittedly, Gosport offers limited points of interest. Though they do have more beachfront on offer than Portsmouth, and in addition the submarine museum that will feature next. Overall, for a few pounds return it is a fun little trip to take, especially for those of you that enjoy being out on the water.

The ferry takes you right to the top of Gosport high street where you will find a market set up on Tuesdays and Saturdays (not exactly a highlight - a very average British high street market where you can buy meat, sweets, phone cases etc.). A good idea for a day trip would be to get the ferry over and have a coffee or lunch in Gosport before returning. There is a popular café situated right opposite the jetty called Coffee#1, or the highly rated Boat House Café that is located a short walk away in the Gosport Marina.

15. EXPLORE SOME UNDERWATER HISTORY

The Submarine museum is actually located in Gosport, rather than Portsmouth, but it is very accessible from Portsmouth, and is one of the main attractions in the area. It is a 20 minute drive from

Portsmouth; alternatively you can get the Gosport Ferry and walk 10 minutes up the road; or if you have purchased an All Attraction Ticket in the dockyard then you can catch the waterbus from there, which goes direct to the submarine museum via Explosion museum.

At the museum, you are able to go on board HMS Alliance, Britain's only WW2 era surviving submarine, where you will meet a veteran submariner who can tell you all about life below the sea. There are three submarines there in total and other artefacts to see in the museum. Even if you believe yourself to have absolutely no interest in submarines, I would highly recommend visiting, as getting to go inside the space where so many people have lived and worked in such a unique way is a fantastic experience that I am confident will interest everyone.

16. ENJOY PRIME SUNSET VIEWS FROM THE COMFORT OF A PUB

Old Portsmouth is a wonderful little corner of the city that fits its descriptive name perfectly. It is the little peninsular to the south of Portsmouth that you will see sticking out into the harbour. Walk down narrow cobbled streets of tightly packed old houses until you get to The Point at the end of the peninsular.

There are two great pubs on The Point which are always packed, inside and out, on summer evenings. It is a perfect location as you face west over the water and therefore get the best view of the sunset. There is always plenty going on out on the water as well, as you are overlooking the entrance to the harbour.

This is a great spot for a cold drink outside; people often sit along all along the sea wall. The pubs also offer good food options, making this a great spot for either lunch or dinner with an engaging view.

17. TAKE A DAY TRIP TO THE ISLE OF WIGHT

The Isle of Wight lies just across the water from Portsmouth, and the Wightlink ferries depart from and arrive at Portsmouth Harbour. A visit to the Isle of Wight would make a good day trip, and is even better if you can spare two or three days to stay over there.

There are many reasons to visit the Isle of Wight, my favourite would be the impression of stepping back in time that you get when you arrive on the island. The island way of life is prevalent and everything seems a bit simpler.

The passenger ferry from Portsmouth takes you to Ryde, where you can either walk all the way down the pier to the island, or you can take the fun option of catching the train. Yes, there is a train station at the end of the pier! The train is made up of disused London Underground carriages and will save you the long walk to town.

The Isle of Wight is famous for being rich in dinosaur remains and fossils. In fact, it is one of the richest areas for dinosaur discovery in the whole of Europe. There is a dinosaur museum on the island if you wish to learn more.

Another highlight of the Island is the Garlic Farm, although perhaps not recommended if you are not keen on garlic. You can visit and explore the actual farm where it is possible to taste and purchase; garlic beer, hot garlic sauce, garlic ice cream, and many other interesting condiments and products. There are also garlic bread making workshops, a garlic inspired restaurant, and tractor trailer tours (just during school holidays). The Garlic Festival happens in mid-August each year.

18. TAKE A GUIDED WALK AROUND THE AREA

There are many guided walks available in Portsmouth from Portsmouth Tourism Guiding Service; and they tend to change yearly so have a search online when you arrive if this is something that interests you. The Nelson trail follows the last steps of Admiral Nelson before he boarded the HMS Victory, perfect for anyone interested in naval history. I recommend the Spice Island tour as a good introduction to Portsmouth and its history.

You can also follow the Renaissance Trail, which is a self-guided walk around the Millennium Promenade. You just need to follow the chain in the pavement, and there will also be information about what you're seeing along the way. The chain takes you along the waterfront from Old Portsmouth, through Gunwharf Quays, and finishes at the Historic Dockyard.

Evening ghost walks run through the summer where you can immerse yourself in the darker side of historical Portsmouth. Set in the early 1800s you will hear all about the underworld of smugglers, prostitutes and pirates. Bad behaviour was rife in Portsmouth with all of those sailors around!

It is also possible to hire a talking guide from the Visitor Information Service, which will give you historical details and points of interest as you walk around.

Portsmouth Guildhall is an impressive venue in the middle of Guildhall Square, and tours of the building are available free of charge.

Lastly, if you are walking around Southsea then keep your eye out for the numerous blue plaques on display. The plaques are there in tribute to some of the well-known former residents including; Sherlock Holmes, Sir Arthur Conan Doyle, Rudyard Kipling and Peter Sellers.

19. CATCH A GAME OF FOOTBALL AT FRATTON PARK

Fratton Park is an institution in Portsmouth. It is the original home of the city's football team, Pompey, and remains so to this day. Relocations have been suggested since the 90s, as many other football teams playing at the same level have acquired new sites or new stadiums, but for various reasons this has not yet happened, and there are currently no relocation plans. The South Stand is the oldest stand still in use, having been built in the 1920s.

Football is arguably the most popular sport in the UK, and also one of the things that we are known for. When I am travelling and locals learn that I am British, they often ask if I come from Manchester, Arsenal, Chelsea, or whatever their favourite British football team is!

Pompey have had their share of success, but in 2012 they were relegated and eventually dropped down to the bottom tier. The football club is now fan owned, and they are working their way back up the rankings, having come first in League Two in May 2017. There are plenty of opportunities for you to watch Pompey play at Fratton Park, just head online or phone up to book a ticket.

20. WHERE TO GO SHOPPING IF YOU AREN'T SO INTERESTED IN DESIGNER LABELS

If you are in town to do a bit of shopping, but not with the same high budget required for Gunwharf Quays, then Commercial Road is where you want to head.

Commercial Road is a typical British high street, featuring branches of many chain stores, alongside a few independent shops. For very cheap clothes and knick-knacks, Primark is hard to beat. It is located within the Cascades shopping centre, where you will also find the wonderfully ethical cosmetics and toiletries shop, Lush.

There are lots of shops and department stores to wander between, interspersed very well with plenty of cafés. Scoops Gelato is a popular ice cream parlour located along the high street, where they serve their famous heavily loaded waffles.

21. HAVE A BEACH DAY

Hayling Island lies to the east of Portsmouth and is accessible by car over the bridge connecting it to the mainland. It is also possible to get a ferry from Eastney, in Portsmouth, to Hayling Island for foot passengers and cyclists.

Hayling Island has a brilliant beach running the width of the island, which is very popular in the summer months and school holidays. The beach is naturally sandy but has had some shingle placed on top of it to protect the land from erosion and flooding. The sea is perfect for swimming and activities such as paddle boarding as the sandbanks running along the coast line make it sheltered and shallow. Hayling island is well known for water sports such as sailing, but especially for windsurfing as it is actually the site where windsurfing was invented!

In addition to the beach, there is a highly rated golf course, and the ever-popular amusement park Funland, which is open all year round.

22. GO FOR A RUN

For some free (and healthy!) entertainment, why not go for a run on the fastest (it's nice and flat) 10km route in the world! Portsmouth provides plenty of good quality flat road surfaces for anyone that enjoys running.

There are many running and walking routes available to view online if you search for 'running Portsmouth'. Portsmouth joggers club are the friendly local jogging club, with hundreds of members and consequently runners of all abilities.

23. GET YOUR SKATES ON

If you are visiting Portsmouth in the winter time then you should visit the ice rink on Guildhall Square to have a go at ice skating.

Portsmouth Guildhall is an impressive historical building sitting on one side of the pedestrian square. The square is beautifully decorated for the festive season with fairy lights, and the big highlight - the ice rink - covering half of the square (646m²).

The other half of the square is made up of alpine style huts containing food wagons, and even an alpine chalet which has a bar inside. An ice skating session, paired with some food and drink, in a picturesque setting, makes for a lovely day out.

24. LET OUT YOUR INNER CHILD ON THE AMUSEMENT PIERS

There are two piers in Portsmouth; South Parade Pier, which sits further west along the coast and Clarence Pier, which is located in Southsea.

Southsea is a classic British seaside resort, with a creative and independent feel to the shops and community that I think makes it particularly special. The fun-centre of the resort has to be the pier which is a staple component of a great seaside resort.

Clarence Pier doesn't actually go very far out into the sea, instead running mostly along the coast. On arrival, you will see the very distinctive blue and yellow tower, which has an amusement arcade and coffee shop on the ground floor, the top floor is home to Pirate Pete's Indoor Adventure Playground, and currently a Wimpy Express fast food restaurant.

There are lots of rides located on the waterfront behind the tower; including a carousel, a circus train, a balloon wheel, dodgems, and many more. One ride that has been there since the pier's inception is the Skyways roller coaster. The funfair has free admission and you just purchase tokens to go on the rides.

South Parade Pier is a pleasure pier that has an amusement arcade, ice creams and a café. It is more reminiscent of a traditional British pier than Clarence Pier as it stretches out into the sea - perfect for wandering up and down.

Helena Cochran

25. SEE SOUTHSEA'S VERY OWN BEACH

Of course, the other highlight of a seaside resort has to be the beach. Southsea has a mainly stony beach, so perhaps not as picturesque as some beaches, but you will get some sand at low tide, and there is a great promenade running along the beach that is perfect for strolling along. The beach has a great view across the Solent to the Isle of Wight, and there are always boats coming and going from the harbour to watch.

The beach isn't very long as it slopes down to the sea quite quickly, but there is still plenty of space for sunbathing - the beach is always popular on sunny days. If you're feeling brave then go for a swim too, some people swim there all year round!

Behind the beach is a canoe lake in a recreation area. The shallow lake is filled with seawater and is therefore a good place for trying some crabbing. You can also have some fun in one of the swan or duck shaped pedalos.

26. GO BRUNCHING AT SOUTHSEA BEACH CAFÉ

While on Southsea seafront, the Southsea Beach Café is a must visit in the local area. It is actually located right opposite the South Parade Pier so you can give that a visit at the same time.

Southsea Beach Café is particularly recommended for breakfast, or for coffee and cake. Check out their Instagram (@southseacafé) if you want to take a peek. They have wonderful views as they are situated right on the beach front, and they offer a full menu including breakfast, sandwiches, dinner, alcoholic drinks and smoothies. They even have ice creams for dogs! There is something on offer no matter what you are after.

27. BECOME KING OF THE (SOUTHSEA) CASTLE

The area of Southsea actually gets its name from Southsea Castle, which was originally constructed in 1544 by Henry VIII. Over the years it has been used as fortification, as a military prison and even had a lighthouse built on it (which is still used for shipping to this day). The castle is small but is located right on the seafront.

Southsea Castle is open to visitors and free to enter in the summer months - between March and October each year. If you are visiting at this time then it is well worth a look. As well as exploring the historical site, you can visit the on-site microbrewery for some beer to take away with you.

Check the event programme before you go as they often offer family trails and other special events. Additionally, from May to September they run their popular Friday Night Champagne Bar. Champagne, in a castle… treat yourself!

If you really want to feel like a king then you can also pay a visit to the Southsea Miniature Village. The village is 1/12th sized and is set inside an old Victorian fort. The village features houses, a railway, forts and even a waterfall.

28. PAY A VISIT TO THE TRANSFORMED HOTWALLS STUDIOS

The Hotwalls are the result of a project completed in 2016 to restore and bring use to the former military barracks located between the Square Tower and the Round Tower on the waterfront.

They have created 13 studios for new and established artists, designers and makers. The studios are all glass fronted so that the public can watch the artists at work.

Hotwalls studios foster a welcoming and creative atmosphere and when the artists are in their studios it is possible to drop by to either explore their space, see what they're working on, or purchase something from the studio. Many of them also offer workshops and commissions and they are always happy to meet people and talk about their art.

29. GRAB A BITE TO EAT IN THE CANTEEN

Alongside the 13 studios in the Hotwalls development, there is also an eatery called The Canteen. The Canteen is located in the bottom of the tower in the middle of the converted arches, which is an awesome location. It is open to the square of Hotwalls studios on one side - perfect for some people watching - and open to the sea on the other.

The old walls containing The Canteen have been renovated particularly well to make the most of the seafront location. You can choose to either sit inside (there are a few really comfy armchairs on offer), or outside on the small decking that sticks out over the sea. Be warned though - you will get wet if you sit there on a windy day, especially at high tide!

The food offerings are in the style of a deli - they have a counter piled high with baked goods and salads, all made from local, seasonal produce. During the winter, it operates as a café, but from May to September they stay open later, until 9pm, where you can enjoy wine, beer and platters.

30. SUPPORT SOME INDEPENDENT BUSINESSES, AND MAYBE EVEN CATCH A FESTIVAL

Albert Road in Southsea is known as an institution of Portsmouth. The street is packed full of independent shops and cafés, and nurtures a creative vibe that attracts so many people that it even has its own Facebook page (Love Albert Road has almost 8,000 likes).

One of the things that Albert Road is known for is its takeaways and restaurants - particularly Chinese or Indian. Albert Road is also popular for a night out and when your night is done you will have to face the impossible choice of Ken's Kebab or Charcoal Grill for your après-drinking snack. The two kebab shops face each other across the street but are surrounded by debate over which is better. This is a decision that you will have to make.

On Albert Road you will also find: tattoo artists; independent skate brands; the most crowded bookshop you have ever been in; and legendary music venue, The Wedgewood Rooms. The Wedgewood Rooms have hosted many big names in their time, despite their limited floor space. It is an independent venue and has been named as one of the top 50 gig venues in the UK by GIGWISE. More on that later...

Another icon on Albert Road is Dress Code; 'an emporium of alternative and vintage' it is an independent specialist vintage boutique and record store. They sell studded things, quirky things, and punk things, among their wide selection that caters to apparently every subculture in existence.

Albert Road is also home to not just one but three festivals. Firstly, Icebreaker is held in various venues on and around Albert Road in February each year. Icebreaker is the 'South's Largest Unsigned Metropolitan Music Festival' - basically, a cheap and fun way to see some up and coming musicians, whilst in a city. Loco Fest is held on Southsea Bandstand and Albert Road in July and showcases the best up and coming local acts. Southsea Fest is the biggest and most successful festival based on Albert Road. The festival takes place in October each year, and they have a dozen stages up and down the road, and around 100 bands and artists playing.

31. PAY A VISIT TO THE MOST ALTERNATIVE RECORD STORE AROUND

Pie and Vinyl is a unique concept, located on Albert Road. The clue is in the name; a record store where people gather to discover and discuss music over a British staple; excellent pie and mash.

Pie and Vinyl are setting a great example of a local business supporting other local businesses and the community. Even their furniture has all been sourced from around Portsmouth and Southsea.

As well as a wide selection of vinyl records, Pie and Vinyl have an interest in music poster art, which they display on their walls and have stock of in the back of the shop. They can get them framed for you with the help of Southsea Gallery.

They have a very extensive pie menu, with some unique flavours. The thing most worth noting is their wide variety of vegetarian, vegan and gluten free options - both in the pies and the sides. The drinks menu is almost as exciting; they have a long list of cordials which are served in a novelty teapot, either cold or warm, alongside speciality coffees, hot chocolate, and lots of options of loose leaf tea blends.

32. THE MOST PORTSMOUTH BRAND YOU WILL FIND

Strong Island is a brand founded in Portsmouth, about Portsmouth, by two creatives who were sick of missing out on events in their own city. It started with a way to keep track of happenings around Portsmouth and has since grown to a creative brand with a blog, a clothes label and store, and a record label.

If you are in Southsea, then you should drop by their shop on Albert Road to take a look at their clothing and accessories. Expect t-shirts printed with Portsmouth loving slogans such as "the sun always shines in Southsea", alongside locally sourced accessories and mugs bearing similar slogans.

Their main aim still remains the same; to keep people informed about the arts and cultural scene in Portsmouth. If you are interested in this side of the city then make sure to either follow Strong Island on social media, or visit their website to see a definitive guide to what's going on and what's worth going to.

33. GO FOR A SWIM IN A PYRAMID

The Pyramids Centre is the big, blue, glass pyramid that you might have spotted on Southsea seafront. It is quite unmissable! The Pyramids are a great family destination as they really pack in the fun for the kids. They have pool inflatables, a wave machine and fun flumes… and that's just in the swimming pools! In addition, there is a three-level soft play area with mazes, ball pits and more.

The Pyramids are also a good adult destination, with a variety of leisure pools as well as a gym, and studios offering classes like yoga. There is also an in-house spa with a sauna, steam room, salt grotto, ice fountain, foot spa, and trained spa therapists offering treatments.

As well as a leisure facility, the Pyramids also acts as a live music venue from time to time. They have had some big names play there, including Coldplay, Arctic Monkeys and Muse.

34. STEP BACK IN TIME AT THE D-DAY MUSEUM

The D-Day Museum is also located along the seafront in Southsea, and at the time of writing is undergoing an extensive refurbishment. It will re-open to the public in February 2018 following a £4.8 million investment.

The museum was opened by the Queen Mother in 1984. The previous centrepiece of the museum was the Overlord Embroidery, which is 272 feet long and is the largest tapestry of its kind in the world - actually the museum was originally built to house the tapestry.

When it reopens, it will have completely new displays about D-Day and the Battle of Normandy. Already a popular visitors' destination, it will definitely be worth a visit when it reopens; take advantage of the recent spending! Especially relevant for any history buffs.

35. ATTEND A BIG BRITISH SUMMER FESTIVAL

Victorious Festival is held over a weekend at the end of August each year. Having previously been just the Saturday and Sunday, in 2017 the festival added a Friday night as well. Camping is not available on site, but they have added camping at Farlington Playing Fields. If you are planning to attend, then I would recommend getting an Air BnB or a hotel room rather than the campsite as it is far away from the festival, and the shuttle buses do not tend to run very late.

The festival has humble beginnings, and is still fairly new. The first festival was in 2011 and held in the Historic Dockyard, with relatively unknown acts headlining. After two years there, they moved to the Castle Fields and Southsea Common, which is a much bigger site, and the acts have been getting bigger and better from there.

2017 saw Madness, Stereophonics, Elbow, The Charlatans, Rita Ora and Olly Murs headline. So far for 2018 they have just announced the first of the Friday night acts, which includes The Kaiser Chiefs and The Libertines. If you can plan your trip to Portsmouth around the festival then I would recommend doing so, particularly with the line-ups going from strength to strength, and the cost of a ticket still relatively low compared to other UK festivals. There are not many festivals where you can watch the sunset on the beach whilst listening to live music - especially in the UK!

The festival site itself is also worth a day of exploring. It encompasses the D-Day museum, the skatepark and other local attractions. There is also a huge array of temporary shops and food stalls, alongside a lot of picturesque seafront.

36. CONSUME SOME GUILT-FREE CAKE

A personal recommendation of where to go for brunch, cake and really great coffee in Southsea. Southsea Coffee Co. is located on Osborne Road and is beautifully decorated inside. They have lots of comfy and cosy seating, and an amazing plant based 'living wall' made by luvshifting which is changed every month or two.

They are a café with sustainability at their heart. Their passion is coffee; they serve speciality coffee, the beans are from micro roasters, and a variety of plant based milks are available as well as the cow's milk which is sourced from a family run farm 20 minutes down the road. On the first Wednesday of every month, they run coffee cuppings. If you are not a coffee drinker, then they have a great loose-leaf tea menu, and delicious hot chocolates.

The food is predominantly a healthy fare, with many veggie and vegan options, but there are always some more indulgent options available.

The cakes are all baked in house, and they have formed their own brand of raw, vegan, gluten free cakes called Ginger and Peach, which are absolutely delicious. If you would like to take something away with you, then the pantry sells their homemade granola, honeycomb butter, coffee and tea.

37. WHERE TO GO FOR SOME FUN IN THE SUN

A BBQ on Southsea Common is a rite of passage for Portsmouth locals and visitors alike. If you are blessed with good weather (which I am confident that you will be, as Southsea tends to have a very pleasant little microclimate) then you will notice that the big, flat, green fields stretching from the seafront to the main road that make up Southsea common are the place to be.

At the first sign of sunshine, people flock to the common; set up picnic blankets, throw frisbees around and set up their little portable BBQs. Portable BBQs are a popular choice in England and can be purchased pretty cheaply from any supermarket or general store. They come with charcoal in a metal tray and just need to be lit and left to burn long enough to get the charcoals hot.

Another sunny day ritual on the common is a game of rounders. If you are reading this from another country, then you may not be familiar with rounders. It is basically the English version of baseball - slower, simpler, and almost exclusively played for fun rather than competitively. The game originates from Tudor times (1700s)!

38. LET YOUR COMPETITIVE SIDE OUT WITH SOME FRIENDLY ROUNDS OF MINI GOLF

Another activity that, to me, is the epitome of a British seaside trip is a good bit of mini golf. There are two mini golf courses to choose from in Portsmouth. The first is Treasure Island Adventure Golf, which has been going for 15 years and has two 9-hole courses named the Warrior and Victory after Portsmouth's resident historic ships. They are located on Southsea Seafront, opposite the fairground rides on Clarence Pier.

As the name suggests, the course is pirate themed, and there is lots to see while you go around. The course goes on to boats, under waterfalls and through caves. This is a fun way to spend an hour or so, and suitable for people of all ages. A little tip is that you can win a free game if you manage to pot your ball in the mini-game by the entrance. The free game voucher is valid forever!

The other option is Southsea Mini Golf, which has a wider array of courses to choose from. There is an 18-hole crazy golf, and 18 hole putting greens. There is also a 9-hole pitch and putt available. Pitch and putt is bigger than crazy golf, and more straightforward, but much more compact than a normal golf course.

39. WHERE TO CELEBRATE YOUR HOLE IN ONE

The Tenth Hole Tea Rooms are just down the road in Southsea, and they also have a 9-hole pitch and putt course. The course ranges from 50 to 91 metre holes. The tea rooms have been under the current management for the last 6 years but the pitch and putt was founded in 1914 which actually makes it the oldest pitch and putt in the world!

The Tenth Hole may be named after the golf, but it is famous in its own right for its extremely instagrammable cakes and overloaded milkshakes (@thetenthhole). In fact, it is probably the most popular tea rooms in Portsmouth, and it is known to have queues outside the door. Not to worry if you do find yourself queuing for a short while though - the friendly servers are known to bring out cake tasters to waiting customers.

They have seating available outside and in, so it is a good spot whatever the weather. I also favour businesses that endeavour to use local suppliers, and the Tenth Hole do just that. All of the cakes from their incredibly vast selection are made in house as well, including their vegan chocolate cake - yum!

40. GET WET, WITH STYLE

The South Coast Wakepark is a water sports activity centre. They offer cable wakeboarding, SUP (stand up paddle boarding), kayaking and raft building.

The Wakepark is largely said to be the South Coast's best cable system, with the extra length making it perfect for beginners to learn to wakeboard on. There are also a few nice obstacles, and friendly coaches on hand throughout your visit who will ensure that you get the most out of your session in the water.

If you want something a bit more laid back, then a go on a SUP is a good option. And if you have good enough balance then you don't even need to get wet!

South Coast Wakepark also have a café on site so you can enjoy a nice cup of tea or coffee, either while watching others get wet, or to warm up after your own trip!

Helena Cochran

41. WHERE TO GO TO CATCH A THEATRE SHOW

A classic cultural diversion is a trip to the Theatre; Portsmouth has three beautiful theatres with active programmes running.

The Kings Theatre in Portsmouth is a cultural highlight of Portsmouth, as well as being one of the working theatres. It was built in 1907 and was designed by the architect Frank Matcham, alongside New Theatre Royal which is also in Portsmouth. The Kings Theatre building is Grade Two listed and has had many restorations over the years, most recently in 2009. Almost all of the original Edwardian features remain, and it is therefore one of the best examples of this style to be found in the British Isles. The Kings Theatre is one of the biggest venues in Portsmouth so has a great range of shows, productions, exhibitions and art showing. They also run behind-the-scenes tours, where you have the chance to see what happens behind the action, and see parts of the theatre not normally accessible to the public.

The other Frank Matcham designed theatre in Portsmouth, the New Theatre Royal was first built in 1761 and known first as Portsmouth Theatre, then Portsmouth and Portsea Theatre, and finally Theatre Royal. Frank Matcham redesigned and enlarged the theatre in 1900 and it has been through many changes since then. Fun fact: the first ever live cookery show was on stage here in 1951! They also run one-hour tours - New Theatre Royal Uncovered - where you can discover the secrets of this historic venue.

Thirdly, we have the Groundlings Theatre, built in 1784. The Georgian theatre is apparently haunted by ten friendly ghosts, and features many secret rooms and hidden doors. Queen Victoria was historically a regular visitor to the theatre. It has recently been fully restored and is now full of life with regular shows running alongside events and a drama school.

42. ROCK OUT TO SOME LIVE MUSIC

Portsmouth is well known for its live music scene. There are some legendary music venues around the city; first and foremost, The Wedgewood Rooms. The Wedgewood Rooms have kept themselves relevant to the music scene for more than 20 years and despite being a small venue, they continue to maintain their legendary reputation.

The Wedgewood Rooms aim to promote new talent, particularly local acts, and the smaller sister venue, The Edge, is used to offer a space to such artists. They have had many success stories of new bands gaining popularity and getting to go on tour with established acts.

The Wedgewood Rooms and The Edge are also known for comedy, theatre, film and spoken word. The Wedge is Portsmouth's oldest comedy club and takes place on Friday nights at The Wedgewood Rooms. Some of the biggest names in comedy have played or started their careers at The Wedge. Food is served for the first hour of the comedy club, and the evening is followed by the retro disco that is almost as well known as the comedy club itself.

Further to The Wedgewood Rooms, Portsmouth is home to some large venues such as The Pyramids Centre and The Guildhall. All in all, Portsmouth holds its own as a live music (and other performances) destination.

43. THE PLACE TO LEARN ALL ABOUT THE CITY'S HISTORY

Portsmouth Museum is definitely worth a visit while you are in the city. The museum has free entry, and free parking to the left of the building. It is set in a beautiful old building and has a range of permanent and temporary collections.

The museum has exhibitions of archaeology, art, Charles Dickens, local history, military history, and natural science. Since Portsmouth was the home of Sherlock Holmes creator Sir Arthur Conan Doyle, you will also find a couple of Sherlock themed permanent displays. In addition, there are two displays about Portsmouth; The Story of Portsmouth explores life in Portsmouth through the generations, while No Place Like Pompey looks at what makes Portsmouth unique.

The museum has a small shop and a café on-site. The shop focuses on local history and local arts and crafts. They also have a wide range of books available to browse and buy. The proceeds from the café go towards supporting the museum.

On a sunny day, swing by to spend some time in the gardens. The museum has a range of garden games that are available to borrow and play with in the grounds. It is free to borrow them, but they currently ask for a £5 deposit.

44. SEE THE BIRTHPLACE OF A LITERARY LEGEND

The other museum that should be on your list for your time in Portsmouth is Charles Dickens' Birthplace Museum. Portsmouth has acquired the title of the Home of Great Writing, due to its involvement in the lives and works of so many famous writers. Charles Dickens' early life was spent in Portsmouth, which makes him the city's most successful writer.

Dickens was born in 1812, at 1 Mile End Terrace (now 393 Old Commercial Road), which is now open to the public. It is a small terraced house but three of the rooms are furnished and faithfully restored to the Regency style of the time. The museum also holds a small collection of memorabilia.

From April to September, there are readings of a selection of Charles Dickens' works on the first Sunday of each month. Held at 3pm there is no extra cost and they last for about 45 minutes. On the 2nd and 4th Saturday of the month, volunteers will be in costume at the museum.

45. GET STUCK INTO A GOOD BOOK, OR TWO...

Portsmouth's extensive literary connections make it a natural place for a festival of books. Portsmouth Bookfest happens each year in February and runs for about two weeks. The idea of the festival is to encourage people to buy and borrow books, particularly those who would be less likely to do so.

2018 will be the 8th year of the book festival, and a long programme of events has been released. Bookfest like to work with local writing talent, and host many workshops for authors or for children, ranging from screen writing to comics. A number of teddy bears picnics are held in the libraries around Portsmouth, where children hear stories, rhymes and complete an activity - all accompanied by a glass of squash and a cupcake!

In addition, Portsmouth University hosts debates and talks with authors and other knowledgeable figures, on a range of current issues. Bookfest also coincides with the artists open studios weekend in the Hotwalls Studios in Old Portsmouth; this provides the opportunity to meet makers and artists, and to see them at work.

In partnership with Bookfest, the contemporary art gallery Aspex, in Gunwharf Quays, is holding an Artist Book Event. The event will feature artists, performers, poets and the public who will explore the link between the written narrative and the visual structures of the books.

46. SEE THE SKIES COME TO LIFE WITH SOME OF THE BEST KITES IN THE WORLD

The annual Portsmouth International Kite Festival has been running since 1991, having had its 25-year anniversary in 2016. It is one of the most popular kite events in the UK; growing year on year since it started. It has actually been listed as one of the best kite festivals in the world. The event is held over two days in mid-August on Southsea Common, and during this time the skies above the common will be filled with a beautiful array of kites.

The event is free to attend, and the variety of kites on the ground and in the air, is wonderfully diverse and creative. Each year has a theme, and kite flyers come from all around the world to attend. A new world record for the number of Trilobite kites flown together was set in 2016 (since lost to America, but the festival hopes to claim it back).

The event always has first time flyers visiting, alongside the world experts, so it is worth dropping by if you are in Portsmouth at the time. The conditions on the common are perfect for flying kites, particularly with the sea breeze. There are synchronised kite flying displays, fighting kites, kite designers, and many more things going on at the event - making it a fun way to spend a day in Portsmouth.

47. UNLEASH YOUR INNER DETECTIVE

The Spice Island Treasure Trail is a great way to explore Portsmouth. The trail is like real life Murder-Mystery-come-Cluedo, and will keep you moving as you will be walking the self-guided route. The route map is downloadable online from the Treasure Trails website, or you can get a hard copy sent to you.

The trail route goes in a loop and takes you around Old Portsmouth, Gunwharf Quays, and Portsmouth Cathedral. In total the trail is around 2.7 miles long and will take two and a half hours to complete. The trail is suitable for participants of 6 years old and above but it is not aimed only at children - adults should not be put off by the absence of any children in their group! All correct answers from the trail are entered in a monthly cash draw for £100 so you might even win some real treasure. Other than that, it is a great way to learn a bit about the history of Portsmouth, while being outside and active. The treasure hunt will uncover places that tourists would not have discovered otherwise, and that locals probably aren't aware of.

48. GET UP CLOSE AND PERSONAL WITH SOME SEALIFE

A trip to the Blue Reef Aquarium is a great option for anyone with a family in tow. It is located on the Southsea waterfront, and is neighboured by a good fish and chip shop - perfect for lunch on the go.

There is a wide variety of marine life on display at the aquarium. A personal highlight is the underwater tunnel that you can walk through, where sharks and rays swim over and around you. There are more than 40 displays in total, and the otter holt is another great attraction.

There are events running throughout the year, and if you time your visit correctly then you can catch some of the animal feedings and educational talks. The aquarium has a focus on conservation of the oceans and educating the public in this area.

If you visit the Blue Reef Aquarium during the summer, then you can also have some fun in the outdoor pool and play area. Perfect for families!

61

Helena Cochran

49. SEE THE LOCAL CATHEDRALS - THE HIGHEST FORM OF CHRISTIAN CHURCHES

Portsmouth is home to not one but two cathedrals; St Thomas' Anglican Cathedral or The Cathedral Church of St Thomas of Canterbury (known as Portsmouth Cathedral) and St John's Catholic Cathedral.

Portsmouth Cathedral is located on Portsmouth High Street. It was first built as a chapel around the year 1180, dedicated to St Thomas of Canterbury who had been murdered and martyred ten years earlier. The church grew to become a parish church in the 14th century, and then finally a cathedral in the 20th century. The building itself has evolved over the years, with different aspects owing to different centuries. You are welcome to visit to view the architecture, and they also hold art exhibitions from time to time. It is a special building that is steeped in history and the friendly volunteers will be able to tell you more information when you are there.

St John's Catholic Cathedral (or The Roman Catholic Cathedral of St John the Evangelist) was opened in 1882 and as such became the first cathedral to be built in Portsmouth. It was designed by John Crawley, and his partner Joseph Hansom.

In addition to the two cathedrals, The Royal Garrison Church is a historic building very much worth a visit. It was built in 1212 by the Bishop of Winchester and went through many uses prior to being restored to a church. The semi-destroyed building is noticeable if you are in Old Portsmouth as it sits on the field at the start of Southsea Common. It is possible to visit the church but this is dependent on volunteers so it is best to check before visiting. One of the highlights is the 20th century stained glass windows that show scenes from the church's history, alongside some Second World War scenes.

50. ENJOY SOME COUNTRY AIR

The last thing to do if you are in the city is, of course, to escape the city! Portsdown Hill is just a 10-minute drive out of Portsmouth but offers fresh air, countryside walks and plenty of green hills to run around on. The main attraction of Portsdown Hill is the spectacular view across Portsmouth, the South Downs and the sea.

The slopes of the chalk hill are home to a large grassland through which the walking paths wind. Much of this land is a Site of Special Scientific Interest due to its density of flowers which provide an excellent home for bees, butterflies and a variety of birdlife.

In addition, Portsdown Hill is dotted with forts and historic sites. The forts were built in the late 1800s with the intention of protecting Portsmouth from possible attacks over land. There are six forts located on the hill; Fort Fareham, Fort Wallington and Fort Widley are Grade Two listed and are used mainly as industrial estates. Fort Widley is open for tours on summer weekends. Fort Nelson is home to The Royal Armouries museum which is open free of charge and is a Grade One listed building which is the highest designation. Fort Southwick is another Grade One listed building that was sold for housing in 2003. Lastly, Fort Purbrook is home to an activity centre offering activities such as archery, climbing and horse riding.

If you are up on the hill, then you must make sure to visit Mick's famous burger van, parked in the carpark and open 24 hours a day. Mick's Monster Burger is a local legend, and comes with the best views in the area.

TOP REASONS TO BOOK THIS TRIP

History: If there is one thing that Portsmouth really over-delivers on, then I think that it has got to be history. Portsmouth started life as a Naval Port and over the years has been used as a store for explosive weapons, become host to the world's oldest dry dock, and is now considered to be the home of the Royal Navy. Off the water, Portsmouth still delivers, with cathedrals, a beautiful ruined church, and forts galore!

Seaside: I do like to be beside the seaside! Who doesn't? Portsmouth is very unique due to it being a city (and therefore providing significant infrastructure and shopping opportunities), whilst also being on an island and surrounded by coastline. Southsea offers not just one, but two pleasure piers, and embodies the classic British seaside destination. Highlights include: fish and chips on the beach, having your ice cream stolen by a seagull, and riding around a man-made lake on a giant plastic swan.

Inspiration: The other thing that I love about Portsmouth is the creative vibe that it fosters. If you are seeking inspiration in any way, then you are sure to find it when surrounded by independent brands, shops and artists. Albert Road is a mecca of independence!

Helena Cochran

> TOURIST

GREATER THAN A TOURIST

Visit GreaterThanATourist.com:

http://GreaterThanATourist.com

Sign up for the Greater Than a Tourist Newsletter:

http://eepurl.com/cxspyf

Follow us on Facebook:

https://www.facebook.com/GreaterThanATourist

Follow us on Pinterest:

http://pinterest.com/GreaterThanATourist

Follow us on Instagram:

http://Instagram.com/GreaterThanATourist

Helena Cochran

> TOURIST

GREATER THAN A TOURIST

Please leave your honest review of this book on Amazon and Goodreads. Thank you. We appreciate your positive and constructive feedback. Thank you.

Helena Cochran

Printed in Great Britain
by Amazon